THOM GUNN Selected Poems

Edited by August Kleinzahler

THOM GUNN (1929–2004) was educated at Cambridge University and had his first collection of poems, *Fighting Terms*, published while still an undergraduate. He moved to San Francisco in 1954, and taught in American universities for several decades. His last collection was *Boss Cupid* (2000).

AUGUST KLEINZAHLER was born in Jersey City in 1949. He is the author of twelve books of poems, most recently *Sleeping It Off in Rapid City*. He lives in San Francisco.

Also by Thom Gunn

Fighting Terms

The Sense of Movement

My Sad Captains and Other Poems

Selected Poems by Thom Gunn and Ted Hughes

Touch

Moly

Jack Straw's Castle

The Passages of Joy

The Man with Night Sweats

Collected Poems

Boss Cupid

Selected Poems

THOM GUNN **Selected Poems**

Edited by August Kleinzahler

Farrar, Straus and Giroux   New York

Farrar, Straus and Giroux
18 West 18th Street, New York 10011

Introduction and selection copyright © 2007 by August Kleinzahler
Poems copyright © 2007 by The Estate of Thom Gunn
All rights reserved
Printed in the United States of America
Originally published in 2007 by Faber and Faber Limited, Great Britain
Published in the United States by Farrar, Straus and Giroux
First American edition, 2009

Library of Congress Cataloging-in-Publication Data
Gunn, Thom.
    [Poems. Selections]
    Selected poems / Thom Gunn ; poems selected by August Kleinzahler.
       p.   cm.
    ISBN-13: 978-0-374-25859-7 (pbk. : alk. paper)
    ISBN-10: 0-374-25859-7 (pbk. : alk. paper)
    I. Kleinzahler, August.   II. Title.

PR6013.U65A6 2009
821'.914—dc22
                                                                    2008048142

Designed by Jonathan D. Lippincott

www.fsgbooks.com

1   3   5   7   9   10   8   6   4   2

Contents

Introduction

It's now thirty years since the first *Selected* Thom Gunn. The poet one finds in these pages is a quite different quantity from the earlier Thom Gunn. From this distance in time, and with the work of the seventies, eighties and nineties before us, the nature and scale of his achievement, as well as how truly anomalous a poet he really was, come into perspective. It all changes the landscape a bit upon re-consideration.

Gunn is an Elizabethan poet in modern dress. To be sure, an Elizabethan poet passed through many filters, historical, cultural, in-tellectual, not least the filter of Modernism; but it does no harm when thinking of Gunn's poetry to think of Marlowe, Shakespeare, or Jonson transposed to the San Francisco Bay area in the second part of the twentieth century, living through and making poetic record of the raucous, druggy late sixties, through to the "plague" of the late eighties and nineties, and its aftermath. It's an exciting prospect to conjure with. Gunn is an exciting poet.

Thom Gunn enjoyed large success early, which, more than any-thing else, seems to have confused the matter. His literary sources will probably seem remote to the contemporary reader, especially the younger reader. However the weltschmerz of postwar Britain may have diffused into the literary culture, certain tendencies are clearly evident in the early poetry of Gunn and in the work of older contemporaries like Larkin who were grouped together, however ar-tificially, as poets of the Movement.

It was around the time of the original publication of this book [*Fighting Terms*] 1954 or perhaps a little earlier, that I first heard of something called the Movement. To my sur-prise, I also learned that I was a member of it. . . . It origi-nated as a half-joke by Anthony Hartley writing in the

Spectator and then was perpetuated as a kind of journalistic convenience. What poets like Larkin, Davie, Elizabeth Jennings, and I had in common at that time was that we were deliberately eschewing Modernism, and turning back, though not very thoroughgoingly, to traditional resources in structure and method.

(From "My Life Up to Now," collected in
The Occasions of Poetry)

Whatever the consanguinities of style and intent, if there was one writer these poets were trying *not* to sound like, it would have been Dylan Thomas, first and foremost. Reaction had already set in against his overheated rhetoric and what one commentator called his id-Romanticism. Likewise, the New Apocalypse poets who published in *Poetry London* in the forties. These young poets were aiming for a poetry that was tough, lean, smart, and up-to-date. The inclination was strongly nativist, which for Gunn meant the Elizabethans and the ballads, and out of the ballads, Hardy. Of the older living poets Gunn was strongly attracted to Auden, for his wit (in the older sense of the word), mastery of forms, and the fact that he was accessible and of his time.

F. R. Leavis's writings about poetry continue to make for bracing reading, especially on the heels of thirty years of structuralism and post-structuralism. Whether one agrees with him or not, the seriousness and muscular intelligence of his arguments are palpable in the syntax of his essays, as I'm certain they were in the lectures Gunn attended at Cambridge in the early fifties. Leavis argued for a poetry of the waking world, for the movement of modern speech. He favored clear edges, the exercise of intelligence and will. His thrust was away from Romanticism, especially Romanticism's influence on Victorian and Pre-Raphaelite poetry. What Leavis seems to have detested most was the cloudy, languid dreamworld of poetry. And what he championed was a poetry of passionate intellectual interest, bare and subtle, responsive to the age it was written in and expressed in the idiom and rhythms of that age. Sounds modernist, doesn't it? Well, yes and no. In any event, when Gunn's first book came out in 1954, poems he'd written as an undergraduate, the voice and forms were decidedly traditional while the attitudes and subject matter were very *now* for then: in Gunn's case *now* involved existentialism and a rather heroic, alienated self.

The popular line on Gunn's poetry is that his first collection, *Fighting Terms*, and his next, *The Sense of Movement*, established him as one of the young lions among poets of his generation; then he came unglued, rather lost, over the years after his move to the States, and with his 1971 collection, *Moly*, had utterly gone down the tubes. Here is Edward Lucie-Smith from the Penguin collection *British Poetry since 1945*:

> Around 1960, it sometimes seemed as if all the poetry being written in England was being produced by a triple-headed creature called the "Larkin-Hughes-Gunn." Of this triumvirate it is Gunn whose reputation has worn least well. The youngest of the Movement poets, he established himself with his first volume. A mixture of the literary and the violent, this appealed both to restless youth and academic middle-age . . . Afterwards Gunn went to America . . .

Kenneth McLeish, in another Penguin compendium, *Companion to the Arts in the Twentieth Century*, writes:

> On present showing, Gunn is living proof of that sad cliché that first thoughts are always the best . . . His collection, *Fighting Terms*, was one of the best poetry-books of its time: a combination of urgent style and that sparky, intellectual involvement with "issues" . . . Gunn became a professor at Berkeley. He continued to publish . . . [but] only *My Sad Captains* (1961) contains anything to match . . . or remotely rival his own spectacular early work.

Fighting Terms is an extraordinarily accomplished, smart, and precocious performance by a university student. It's difficult to conceive of such a performance today by one so young. There's a real muscularity and rigor in the handling of meter, as well as considerable discipline, rare in one that age, in his control of idea and structure, seeing through to the end the extended metaphors he favored at that time in his work. The poet's enormous gifts are already very much in evidence.

Gunn was twenty-two when he entered university, having completed his National Service and having worked briefly in Paris. There is one especially fine example of his early style in the book "Tamer and Hawk," seamless in execution and convincing all the way through, but the rest of the book reads now as top-of-the-line juvenilia, interesting only with respect to the later work. In truth, very few actually read the book at the time (it was published in an edition of only three hundred copies), but it established his reputation, a reputation amplified and consolidated by *The Sense of Movement*, published by Faber in 1957. Gunn was now famous in England, his work enjoying "a public," insofar as a public was to be found for poetry at the time. However, three years before, Gunn had removed himself to California where he would, as was alleged over and over, begin his long decline, undone by sunshine, LSD, queer sex, and free verse. It will now have taken more than a generation to set the record straight.

The Sense of Movement is a broad advance but still a very long way from the accomplishment of his mature work. Gunn would have been at Stanford when most of these poems were written and studying with Yvor Winters. Winters, like Leavis, was another brilliant, forceful personality. Those types of mentoring individual can be poison for young writers, but Gunn, as he would throughout his writing life, would take what he could use and move along. Part of his talent, or good fortune, from early on, was to make good decisions, often tough ones. Indeed, the writing of a poem involves a series of hard decisions, often daunting ones.

Winters, like Leavis, very much believed in intellectual rigor in poetry, and moral penetration as well. Like Leavis he was serious about literature; it was the most important thing in the world. You get that from the writings of both men. Gunn would continue to pursue his interest in the Elizabethans and their successors, most significantly Jonson and Greville. Winters was at his most brilliant and enthusiastic when discussing the Elizabethans, in particular the shorter Elizabethan lyric.

> I had long liked the Elizabethans. I knew Nashe's few poems well, Ralegh's, and even some of Greville's; Donne had been, after Shakespeare, my chief teacher. So I already shared some

of Winters' tastes, and though I liked the ornate and the metaphysical I needed no persuading to also like the plain style.

("On a Drying Hill: Yvor Winters," from *Shelf Life*)

But Gunn would at this point also be introduced to W. C. Williams and read with more understanding and depth Stevens, Pound, and other Americans that Winters valued. Under Winters's tutelage Gunn would come to understand the logical continuum from poetry of the English Renaissance to the Modernists. It is an understanding and interest that would color his own poetry from that point on.

The writing in *The Sense of Movement* is measurably crisper and more assured than the earlier collection, also less rhetorical. Gunn starts out as a literary writer and remains so throughout his career, but the poetry in Gunn's first few books feels at a remove from the world. Later on his reading and world would come to better inform each other and with great effect, but not quite yet. What does begin to show up clearly in the poetry is Gunn's fascination with the city as subject matter and his use of what is called the Plain Style.

Gunn came to Baudelaire early, before Cambridge, and stayed with him. The poems from *Les Tableaux parisiens* in *Les Fleurs du mal* made as much of an impression on him and his writing as Donne and Shakespeare later would. In fact, it would be difficult to overstate what Gunn drew from the Baudelairean sensibility about cities, in particular the interest in the low, the squalid. In *The Sense of Movement* Gunn has begun to stretch out a bit more, trying out syllabics in a couple of poems, and discover his real subject matter. The city will become his central theme, character and event being played out on its street corners, in its rooms, bars, bathhouses, stairwells, taxis. There is also evidence in the 1957 book that Gunn is beginning, here and there, to relax toward his material, to drop the lofty distanced tone and actually nose around a bit. He's getting interested and the poetry is beginning to get interesting.

The Plain Style is what it sounds to be: unembellished, clear; in diction and movement inclining toward the way people speak. It doesn't call attention to itself but serves the material of the poem. Among the ancients, Horace, in his Epistle to Florus, advises the poet "to master the rhythms and measures of genuine life." Among sixteenth- and seventeenth-century writers the term Plain Style distinguishes itself from the ornamental figures of the Petrarchan Style. Ben Jonson is probably its chief exemplar. Gunn liked no poet better.

The Plain Style, however, is not to be confused with the colloquial. Although transparently an exponent of the Plain Style, Gunn does not sound especially "plain" to the contemporary reader. His diction is lean and unadorned—*chaste*, as the poet Clive Wilmer describes it—the argument and exposition are clear, trim, and direct, but the tone may sound oddly formal to the twenty-first-century reader. He is not trying for the cadences of speech. The meter and rhyme of most of the poetry notwithstanding, the voice tends to feel anachronistic; the "I" of the poetry carrying almost no tangible personality. This can be upsetting or disappointing to the contemporary reader, especially the American reader, accustomed to the dramatic personalities behind the voices in recent poetry: Lowell, Berryman, Sexton, Ginsberg, Plath, Hughes, et al. Even in Larkin there exists a strong, identifiable persona, no matter how recessive the tone.

This absence of personality is by design in Gunn's poetry. The "I" in the poems is the disinterested "I" of the Elizabethans, and back further still, the "I" of the ballads, and out of the ballads the "I" in Hardy's poetry. One can also encounter it in Bunting's "Briggflatts," a poem of major importance to Gunn later on in his career. In an interview, Gunn tells us quite explicitly what he's up to with regard to voice:

> People do have difficulties with my poetry, difficulties in locating the central voice or central personality. But I'm not aiming for central voice and I'm not aiming for central personality. I want to be an Elizabethan poet. I want to write with the same anonymity that you get in the Elizabethans and I want to move around between forms in the same way somebody like Ben Jonson did. At the same time I want to write in my own century.

This stance was to upset many readers and reviewers, who, as Donald Davie remarks in an essay on Gunn, were affronted by Gunn's impersonality, having become accustomed to a rhetorical theory of poetry whereby the writer's prime duty is to serve the reader's rather than the writer's own experience, that reader conceiving of poetry as a "service industry." Davie goes on to say that this perceived impertinence on Gunn's part was aggravated by the nature of the subject matter Gunn was treating—sexual abandon, drugs, etc.—which the reader felt so emotionally about and Gunn treated so coolly. "I distrust myself with rhetoric," Gunn told James Campbell in a late interview, "because it would be a form of falsification."

Which brings us to the next line on Gunn's career: after going to hell in America, squandering his poetic gifts, Gunn was rehabilitated by the AIDS crisis and became an important poet once again because be became a *feeling* poet at last. The truth is that the trajectory of Gunn's career can be easily enough charted and does not at all resemble what the self-perpetuating notions contend. He grows from book to book until he publishes *Moly* in 1971.

You can see it coming, especially in the poems in Part II of *My Sad Captains*, in 1961. Gunn addresses the change in his work in an autobiographical note written for Faber and Faber in November of 1972:

> The first half [of the book] is the culmination of my old style—metrical, rational, but maybe starting to get a little more humane. The second half consists of a taking up of that humaner impulse in a series of syllabic poems . . . which were . . . really only a way of teaching myself to write free verse.

Of the first poem, "In Santa Maria del Popolo," Gunn writes: "Here at last I begin some kind of critique of the heroic."

As splendid as so many of the poems in *My Sad Captains* are, the advance to the plateau of *Moly*, some ten years later, is startling. It's reasonable enough, I suppose, when one considers that Gunn was in his midthirties when he wrote *Moly*. His skills and intelligence were abundantly in evidence up to that point, but to this reader, at least, he was a more accomplished poet than an important one. It's not untoward or irrelevant to speculate on the personal: he'd recently been through a bad bout of hepatitis; he'd quit his full-time teaching job at Berkeley; he'd come out more publicly as a gay man; he'd begun dropping acid. But plenty of artists pass through personal change and crisis and their work is none the better for it; in fact, more often than not the work suffers on account of it.

Moly begins dramatically with a poem of change, metamorphosis. It is one of the thrilling moments in twentieth-century poetry:

> Something is taking place.
> Horns bud bright in my hair.
> My feet are turning hoof.
> And Father, see my face
> —Skin that was damp and fair
> Is barklike and, feel, rough.
>   ("Rites of Passage")

The transformation motif continues through the next poem, the title poem "Moly," and gains tremendous pitch through the movement within its couplets:

> Into what bulk has method disappeared?
> Like ham, streaked. I am gross—grey, gross, flap-eared.
>
> The pale-lashed eyes my only human feature.
> My teeth tear, tear. I am the snouted creature
>
> That bites through anything, root, wire, or can.
> If I was not afraid I'd eat a man.
>
> Oh a man's flesh already is in mine.
> Hand and foot poised for risk. Buried in swine.
>
>   I root and root, you think that it is greed,
> It is, but I seek out a plant I need.
>
> Direct me gods, whose changes are all holy,
> To where it flickers deep in grass, the moly [. . .]

Whatever was left of Gunn's considerable late-fifties reputation in Britain, *Moly* finished it off. One reviewer wrote of the book: "Without exception the *Moly* poems are dead. Their failure is not essentially a failure of tone. They do not *smell*." And when he had sent some of these poems to Yvor Winters in the course of the sixties, his old mentor wrote back that maybe he should try writing prose. Change has a cost, and from Winters himself, had he not known it already, Gunn had had impressed upon him that career means nothing, only one's art and honesty count for anything. As Edwin Muir noted, early in Gunn's career: "He is endowed and plagued by an unusual honesty. His poems are a desperate inquiry, how to live and act in a world perpetually moving."

The mid- to late sixties generated a lot of garbage in the arts, junk that really started piling up in the seventies. A loose man, given as much permission as he wants, will make a very loose poem. The era was a time of gross self-indulgence. Gunn on the other hand flourished: instead of going prolix and slack (listen once more to the ten-minute guitar riffs and saxophone solos of the time) he relaxed into his mature voice. A transformation had taken place.

His poetry could accommodate a bit of relaxing. He will remain preeminently a poet of closure, intelligence, and will, as evidenced in the *Moly* poems. There was not an aleatory bone in Gunn's body. He's Handel, not John Cage. Even in the free verse that becomes a part of his arsenal the procedures are not especially Modernist: not at all elliptical, no collage or fractured syntax, nothing in medias res—none of that. His free-verse poems have a beginning, a middle, and an end. They develop rationally. The diction remains *plain*, the argument direct. His free verse is not at all prosey, and possesses its own kind of subdued music. Gunn owes a considerable debt in the nonmetrical poems to W. C. Williams, especially with regard to Williams's short line and use of enjambment. The subject matter is usually city life, often squalid, his characters the vulnerable, much of it along the lines of Baudelaire's *Les Tableaux parisiens*. The sexual gains increasing prominence in the work: the city for Gunn, specifically San Francisco, becomes a kind of sexual New Jerusalem, a bit seedy around the edges, where the utopian notion of a Whitmanesque brotherhood of man becomes a recurring theme. But what has changed most demonstrably in the poetry in *Moly* and beyond is Gunn's relationship with his environment. We are no longer dealing so much with allegories or notions of the city or character: the poems are now trained on actual people and places. If earlier on in the poetry it seemed as if there was no there there, now the there is very much in evidence.

From this point on another recurrent theme is personal abandon. He likes to treat these subjects, to contain them, in rhyme and meter. Gunn's experiences on LSD had become hugely important and instructive for him, and made their way into his poetry.

> Metre seemed to be the proper form for the LSD-related poems, though at first I didn't understand why. Later I rationalized about it thus. The acid trip is unstructured, it opens you up to countless possibilities, you hanker after the infinite. The only way I could give myself any control over the presentation of these experiences, and so could be true to them, was by trying to render the infinite through the finite, the unstructured through the structured. Otherwise there was the danger of the experience's becoming so distended that it would simply unravel like fog before the wind in the unpremeditated movement of free verse.
>
> ("My Life Up to Now," from *The Occasions of Poetry*)

The poem "At the Centre," from the *Moly* collection, written during an LSD trip on the fenced-in, graveled roof of a Hamm beer brewery, is a wonderful example.

> What is this steady pouring that
> 　　　　　　Oh, wonder.
> The blue line bleeds and on the gold one draws.
> Currents of image widen, braid, and blend
> —Pouring in cascade over me and under—
> To one all-river. Fleet it does not pause,
> The sinewy flux pours without start or end.
>
> What place is this
> 　　　　　　And what is it that broods
> Barely beyond its own creation's course,

And not abstracted from it, not the Word,
But overlapping like the wet low clouds
The rivering images—their unstopped source,
Its roar unheard from being always heard.

It seemed that as a poet Thom Gunn became more adventure-some as he grew older. The intellectual rigor, moral curiosity, and firmness of structure that Gunn brought to his work from the beginning never left him but the poetry itself opened and deepened over time. Gunn himself had grown, "by a cubit's length," as he liked to quote his former Cambridge teacher Helen Shire, of those who had read through Shakespeare with understanding. "Gunn dug further than any of his contemporaries," Donald Davie wrote, "into the English of earlier centuries, so as to recover that phase of English—Donne's, Marlowe's, above all Shakespeare's—in which language could register without embarrassment on the one hand the sleazy and squalid, and on the other hand the affirmative, the frankly heroic."

On the heels of *Moly* come *Jack Straw's Castle*, *The Passages of Joy*, the magisterial *The Man with Night Sweats*, the *Collected Poems*, and finally *Boss Cupid*, this last, containing, among other memorable pieces, "The Gas-poker," the poem about his mother's suicide, a subject it took Gunn over fifty years to engage in verse. Predictably, he chose meter and rhyme to contain this most difficult and troubling episode in his life. The tone of it, as ever, is dispassionate, the voice anonymous, and the pathos of the event all the more powerful on account of it.

The level of achievement from Part II of *My Sad Captains* through to *Boss Cupid* is extraordinary, not least for having been sustained for forty years, years of real neglect for the work both in Britain and America. And during those years Gunn continued to challenge himself through the medium, sometimes stumbling, but never standing pat, and above all trying to make sense of the world, his world, as honestly as possible, steering clear of the rhetorical and self-congratulatory at every turn.

But we might well look to the words of Fulke Greville, writing of his own work, to best characterize Gunn's poetry from the sixties on:

For my own part I found my creeping genius more fixed upon the images of life, than the images of wit, and therefore chose not to write to them on whose foot the black ox had not already trod, as the proverb is, but to those only that are weather-beaten in the sea of this world, such as having lost the sight of their gardens and groves, study to sail on a right course among rocks and quicksands.

AUGUST KLEINZAHLER

from **FIGHTING TERMS** (1954)

The Wound

The huge wound in my head began to heal
About the beginning of the seventh week.
Its valleys darkened, its villages became still:
For joy I did not move and dared not speak,
Not doctors would cure it, but time, its patient skill.

And constantly my mind returned to Troy.
After I sailed the seas I fought in turn
On both sides, sharing even Helen's joy
Of place, and growing up—to see Troy burn—
As Neoptolemus, that stubborn boy.

I lay and rested as prescription said.
Manoeuvered with the Greeks, or sallied out
Each day with Hector. Finally my bed
Became Achilles' tent, to which the lout
Thersites came reporting numbers dead.

I was myself: subject to no man's breath:
My own commander was my enemy.
And while my belt hung up, sword in the sheath,
Thersites shambled in and breathlessly
Cackled about my friend Patroclus' death.

I called for armour, rose, and did not reel.
But, when I thought, rage at his noble pain
Flew to my head, and turning I could feel
My wound break open wide. Over again
I had to let those storm-lit valleys heal.

Tamer and Hawk

I thought I was so tough,
But gentled at your hands,
Cannot be quick enough
To fly for you and show
That when I go I go
At your commands.

Even in flight above
I am no longer free:
You seeled me with your love,
I am blind to other birds—
The habit of your words
Has hooded me.

As formerly, I wheel
I hover and I twist,
But only want the feel,
In my possessive thought,
Of catcher and of caught
Upon your wrist.

You but half civilize,
Taming me in this way.
Through having only eyes
For you I fear to lose,
I lose to keep, and choose
Tamer as prey.

from **THE SENSE OF MOVEMENT** (1957)

On the Move

The blue jay scuffling in the bushes follows
Some hidden purpose, and the gust of birds
That spurts across the field, the wheeling swallows,
Has nested in the trees and undergrowth.
Seeking their instinct, or their poise, or both,
One moves with an uncertain violence
Under the dust thrown by a baffled sense
Or the dull thunder of approximate words.

On motorcycles, up the road, they come:
Small, black, as flies hanging in heat, the Boys,
Until the distance throws them forth, their hum
Bulges to thunder held by calf and thigh.
In goggles, donned impersonality,
In gleaming jackets trophied with the dust,
They strap in doubt—by hiding it, robust—
And almost hear a meaning in their noise.

Exact conclusion of their hardiness
Has no shape yet, but from known whereabouts
They ride, direction where the tyres press.
They scare a flight of birds across the field:
Much that is natural, to the will must yield.
Men manufacture both machine and soul,
And use what they imperfectly control
To dare a future from the taken routes.

It is a part solution, after all.
One is not necessarily discord
On earth; or damned because, half animal,
One lacks direct instinct, because one wakes
Afloat on movement that divides and breaks.
One joins the movement in a valueless world,
Choosing it, till, both hurler and the hurled,
One moves as well, always toward, toward.

A minute holds them, who have come to go:
The self-defined, astride the created will
They burst away; the towns they travel through
Are home for neither bird nor holiness,
For birds and saints complete their purposes.
At worst, one is in motion; and at best,
Reaching no absolute, in which to rest,
One is always nearer by not keeping still.

At the Back of the North Wind

All summer's warmth was stored there in the hay;
Below, the troughs of water froze: the boy
Climbed nightly up the rungs behind the stalls
And planted deep between the clothes he heard
The kind wind bluster, but the last he knew
Was sharp and filled his head, the smell of hay.

Here wrapped within the cobbled mews he woke.
Passing from summer, climbing down through winter
He broke into an air that kept no season:
Denying change, for it was always there.
It nipped the memory numb, scalding away
The castle of winter and the smell of hay.

The ostlers knew, but did not tell him more
Than hay is what we turn to. Other smells,
Horses, leather, manure, fresh sweat, and sweet
Mortality, he found them on the North.
That was her sister, East, that shrilled all day
And swept the mews dead clean from wisps of hay.

High Fidelity

I play your furies back to me at night,
The needle dances in the grooves they made,
For fury is passion like love, and fury's bite,
These grooves, no sooner than a love mark fade;
Then all swings round to nightmare: from the rim,
To prove the guilt I don't admit by day,
I duck love as a witch to sink or swim
Till in the ringed and level I survey
The tuneless circles that succeed a voice.
They run, without distinction, passion, rage,
Around a soloist's merely printed name
That still turns, from the impetus not choice,
Surrounded in that played-out pose of age
By notes he was, but cannot be again.

To Yvor Winters, 1955

I leave you in your garden.
In the yard
Behind it, run the Airedales you have reared
With boxer's vigilance and poet's rigour:
Dog-generations you have trained the vigour
That few can breed to train and fewer still
Control with the deliberate human will.
And in the house there rest, piled shelf on shelf,
The accumulations that compose the self—
Poem and history: for if we use
Words to maintain the actions that we choose,
Our words, with slow defining influence,
Stay to mark out our chosen lineaments.

Continual temptation waits on each
To renounce his empire over thought and speech,
Till he submit his passive faculties
To evening, come where no resistance is;
The unmotivated sadness of the air
Filling the human with his own despair.
Where now lies power to hold the evening back?
Implicit in the grey is total black:
Denial of the discriminating brain
Brings the neurotic vision, and the vein
Of necromancy. All as relative
For mind as for the sense, we have to live
In a half-world, not ours nor history's,
And learn the false from half-true premisses.

But sitting in the dusk—though shapes combine,
Vague mass replacing edge and flickering line,
You keep both Rule and Energy in view,
Much power in each, most in the balanced two:
Ferocity existing in the fence

Built by an exercised intelligence.
Though night is always close, complete negation
Ready to drop on wisdom and emotion,
Night from the air or the carnivorous breath,
Still it is right to know the force of death,
And, as you do, persistent, tough in will,
Raise from the excellent the better still.

from **MY SAD CAPTAINS** (1961)

In Santa Maria del Popolo

Waiting for when the sun an hour or less
Conveniently oblique makes visible
The painting on one wall of this recess
By Caravaggio, of the Roman School,
I see how shadow in the painting brims
With a real shadow, drowning all shapes out
But a dim horse's haunch and various limbs,
Until the very subject is in doubt.

But evening gives the act, beneath the horse
And one indifferent groom, I see him sprawl,
Foreshortened from the head, with hidden face,
Where he has fallen, Saul becoming Paul.
O wily painter, limiting the scene
From a cacophony of dusty forms
To the one convulsion, what is it you mean
In that wide gesture of the lifting arms?

No Ananias croons a mystery yet,
Casting the pain out under name of sin.
The painter saw what was, an alternate
Candour and secrecy inside the skin.
He painted, elsewhere, that firm insolent
Young whore in Venus' clothes, those pudgy cheats,
Those sharpers; and was strangled, as things went,
For money, by one such picked off the streets.

I turn, hardly enlightened, from the chapel
To the dim interior of the church instead,
In which there kneel already several people,
Mostly old women: each head closeted
In tiny fists holds comfort as it can.
Their poor arms are too tired for more than this
—For the large gesture of solitary man,
Resisting, by embracing, nothingness.

Modes of Pleasure (#2)

New face, strange face, for my unrest.
I hunt your look, and lust marks time
Dark in his doubtful uniform,
Preparing once more for the test.

You do not know you are observed:
Apart, contained, you wait on chance,
Or seem to, till your callous glance
Meets mine, as callous and reserved.

And as it does we recognize
That sharing an anticipation
Amounts to a collaboration—
A warm game for a warmer prize.

Yet when I've had you once or twice
I may not want you any more:
A single night is plenty for
Every magnanimous device.

Why should that matter? Why pretend
Love must accompany erection?
This is a momentary affection,
A curiosity bound to end,

Which as good-humoured muscle may
Against the muscle try its strength
—Exhausted into sleep at length—
And will not last long into day.

The Value of Gold

The hairs turn gold upon my thigh,
And I am gold beneath the sun,
Losing pale features that the cold
Pinched, pointed, for an instant I
Turn blind to features, being one
With all that has, like me, turned gold.

I finish up the can of beer,
And lay my head on the cropped grass:
Now bordering flag, geranium,
And mint-bush tower above me here,
Which colour into colour pass
Toward the last state they shall become.

Of insect size, I walk below
The red, green, greenish-black, and black,
And speculate. Can this quiet growth
Comprise at once the still-to-grow
And a full form without a lack?
And, if so, can I too be both?

I darken where perpetual
Action withdraws me from the sun.
Then from one high precocious stalk
A flower—its fulness reached—lets fall
Features, great petals, one by one
Shrivelling to gold across my walk.

Waking in a Newly Built House

The window, a wide pane in the bare
modern wall, is crossed by colourless
peeling trunks of the eucalyptus
recurring against raw sky-colour.

It wakes me, and my eyes rest on it,
sharpening, and seeking merely all
of what can be seen, the substantial,
where the things themselves are adequate.

So I observe them, able to see
them as they are, the neutral sections
of trunk, spare, solid, lacking at once
disconnectedness and unity.

There is a tangible remoteness
of the air about me, its clean chill
ordering every room of the hill-top
house, and convoking absences.

Calmly, perception rests on the things,
and is aware of them only in
their precise definition, their fine
lack of even potential meanings.

Flying above California

Spread beneath me it lies—lean upland
sinewed and tawny in the sun, and

valley cool with mustard, or sweet with
loquat. I repeat under my breath

names of places I have not been to:
Crescent City, San Bernardino

—Mediterranean and Northern names.
Such richness can make you drunk. Sometimes

on fogless days by the Pacific,
there is a cold hard light without break

that reveals merely what is—no more
and no less. That limiting candour,

that accuracy of the beaches,
is part of the ultimate richness.

Considering the Snail

The snail pushes through a green
night, for the grass is heavy
with water and meets over
the bright path he makes, where rain
has darkened the earth's dark. He
moves in a wood of desire,

pale antlers barely stirring
as he hunts. I cannot tell
what power is at work, drenched there
with purpose, knowing nothing.
What is a snail's fury? All
I think is that if later

I parted the blades above
the tunnel and saw the thin
trail of broken white across
litter, I would never have
imagined the slow passion
to that deliberate progress.

The Feel of Hands

The hands explore tentatively,
two small live entities whose shapes
I have to guess at. They touch me
all, with the light of fingertips

testing each surface of each thing
found, timid as kittens with it.
I connect them with amusing
hands I have shaken by daylight.

There is a sudden transition:
they plunge together in a full
formed single fury; they are grown
to cats, hunting without scruple;

they are expert but desperate.
I am in the dark. I wonder
when they grew up. It strikes me that
I do not know whose hands they are.

Lights among Redwood

And the streams here, ledge to ledge,
take care of light. Only to
the pale green ribs of young ferns
tangling above the creek's edge
it may sometimes escape, though
in quick diffusing patterns.

Elsewhere it has become tone,
pure and rarified; at most
a muted dimness coloured
with moss-green, charred grey, leaf-brown.
Calm shadow! Then we at last
remember to look upward:

constant, to laws of size and
age the thick forms hold, though gashed
through with Indian fires. At once
tone is forgotten: we stand
and stare—mindless, diminished—
at their rosy immanence.

of Muir Woods

My Sad Captains

One by one they appear in
the darkness: a few friends, and
a few with historical
names. How late they start to shine!
but before they fade they stand
perfectly embodied, all

the past lapping them like a
cloak of chaos. They were men
who, I thought, lived only to
renew the wasteful force they
spent with each hot convulsion.
They remind me, distant now.

True, they are not at rest yet,
but now that they are indeed
apart, winnowed from failures,
they withdraw to an orbit
and turn with disinterested
hard energy, like the stars.

from **TOUCH** (1967)

The Goddess

When eyeless fish meet her on
her way upward, they gently
turn together in the dark
brooks. But naked and searching
as a wind, she will allow
no hindrance, none, and bursts up

through potholes and narrow flues
seeking an outlet. Unslowed
by fire, rock, water or clay,
she after a time reaches
the soft abundant soil, which
still does not dissipate her

force—for look! sinewy thyme
reeking in the sunlight; rats
breeding, breeding, in their nests;
and the soldier by a park
bench with his greatcoat collar
up, waiting all evening for

a woman, any woman
her dress tight across her ass
as bark in moonlight. Goddess,
Proserpina: it is we,
vulnerable, quivering,
who stay you to abundance.

Touch

You are already
asleep. I lower
myself in next to
you, my skin slightly
numb with the restraint
of habits, the patina of
self, the black frost
of outsideness, so that even
unclothed it is
a resilient chilly
hardness, a superficially
malleable, dead
rubbery texture.

You are a mound
of bedclothes, where the cat
in sleep braces
its paws against your
calf through the blankets,
and kneads each paw in turn.

Meanwhile and slowly
I feel a is it
my own warmth surfacing or
the ferment of your whole
body that in darkness beneath
the cover is stealing
bit by bit to break
down that chill.
                    You turn and
hold me tightly, do
you know who
I am or am I
your mother or

the nearest human being to
hold on to in a
dreamed pogrom.

What I, now loosened,
sink into is an old
big place, it is
there already, for
you are already
there, and the cat
got there before you, yet
it is hard to locate.
What is more, the place is
not found but seeps
from our touch in
continuous creation, dark
enclosing cocoon round
ourselves alone, dark
wide realm where we
walk with everyone.

from **MOLY** (1971)

Rites of Passage

Something is taking place.
Horns bud bright in my hair.
My feet are turning hoof.
And Father, see my face
—Skin that was damp and fair
Is barklike and, feel, rough.

See Greytop how I shine.
I rear, break loose, I neigh
Snuffing the air, and harden
Toward a completion, mine.
And next I make my way
Adventuring through your garden.

My play is earnest now.
I canter to and fro.
My blood, it is like light.
Behind an almond bough,
Horns gaudy with its snow,
I wait live, out of sight.

All planned before my birth
For you, Old Man, no other,
Whom your groin's trembling warns.
I stamp upon the earth
A message to my mother.
And then I lower my horns.

Moly

Nightmare of beasthood, snorting, how to wake.
I woke. What beasthood skin she made me take?

Leathery toad that ruts for days on end,
Or cringing dribbling dog, man's servile friend,

Or cat that prettily pounces on its meat,
Tortures it hours, then does not care to eat:

Parrot, moth, shark, wolf, crocodile, ass, flea.
What germs, what jostling mobs there were in me.

These seem like bristles, and the hide is tough.
No claw or web here: each foot ends in hoof.

Into what bulk has method disappeared?
Like ham, streaked. I am gross—grey, gross, flap-eared.

The pale-lashed eyes my only human feature.
My teeth tear, tear. I am the snouted creature

That bites through anything, root, wire, or can.
If I was not afraid I'd eat a man.

Oh a man's flesh already is in mine.
Hand and foot poised for risk. Buried in swine.

I root and root, you think that it is greed,
It is, but I seek out a plant I need.

Direct me gods, whose changes are all holy,
To where it flickers deep in grass, the moly:

Cool flesh of magic in each leaf and shoot,
From milky flower to the black forked root.

From this fat dungeon I could rise to skin
And human title, putting pig within.

I push my big grey wet snout through the green,
Dreaming the flower I have never seen.

Phaedra in the Farm House

From sleep, before first light,
I hear slow-rolling churns
Clank over flags below.
Aches me. The room returns.
I hurt, I wake, I know
The cold dead end of night.

Here father. And here son.
What trust I live between.
But warmth here on the sheet
Is kin-warmth, slow and clean.
I cook the food two eat,
But oh, I sleep with one.

And you, in from the stable.
You spent last evening
Lost in the chalky blues
Of warm hills, rabbitting.
You frown and spell the news,
With forearms on the table.

Tonight, though, we play cards.
You are not playing well.
I smell the oil-lamp's jet,
The parlour's polished smell,
Then you—soap, ghost of sweat,
Tractor oil, and the yards.

Shirt-sleeved you concentrate.
Your moleskin waistcoat glints
Your quick grin never speaks:
I study you for hints
—Hints from those scrubbed boy-cheeks?

I deal a grown man's fate.
The churns wait on in mud:
Tomorrow's milk will sour.
I leave, but bit by bit,
Sharp through the last whole hour.
The chimney will be split,
And that waistcoat be blood.

Three

All three are bare.
The father towels himself by two grey boulders
    Long body, then long hair,
Matted like rainy bracken, to his shoulders.

The pull and risk
Of the Pacific's touch is yet with him:
    He kicked and felt it brisk,
Its cold live sinews tugging at each limb.

It haunts him still:
Drying his loins, he grins to notice how,
    Struck helpless with the chill,
His cock hangs tiny and withdrawn there now.

Near, eyes half-closed,
The mother lies back on the hot round stones,
    Her weight to theirs opposed
And pressing them as if they were earth's bones.

Hard bone, firm skin,
She holds her breasts and belly up, now dry,
    Striped white where clothes have been,
To the heat that sponsors all heat, from the sky.

Only their son
Is brown all over. Rapt in endless play,
    In which all games make one,
His three-year nakedness is everyday.

Swims as dogs swim.
Rushes his father, wriggles from his hold.
    His body which is him,
Sturdy and volatile, runs off the cold.

        Runs up to me:
Hi there hi there, he shrills, yet will not stop,
    For though continually
Accepting everything his play turns up

        He still leaves it
And comes back to that pebble-warmed recess
    In which the parents sit,
At watch, who had to learn their nakedness.

Words

The shadow of a pine-branch quivered
On a sunlit bank of pale unflowering weed.
   I watched, more solid by the pine,
The dark exactitude that light delivered,
     And, from obsession, or from greed,
       Laboured to make it mine.

   In looking for the words, I found
Bright tendrils, round which that sharp outline faltered:
   Limber detail, no bloom disclosed.
I was still separate on the shadow's ground
     But, charged with growth, was being altered,
       Composing uncomposed.

From the Wave

It mounts at sea, a concave wall
    Down-ribbed with shine,
And pushes forward, building tall
    Its steep incline.

Then from their hiding rise to sight
    Black shapes on boards
Bearing before the fringe of white
    It mottles towards.

Their pale feet curl, they poise their weight
    With a learn'd skill.
It is the wave they imitate
    Keeps them so still.

The marbling bodies have become
    Half wave, half men,
Grafted it seems by feet of foam
    Some seconds, then,

Late as they can, they slice the face
    In timed procession:
Balance is triumph in this place,
    Triumph possession.

The mindless heave of which they rode
    A fluid shelf
Breaks as they leave it, falls and, slowed,
    Loses itself.

Clear, the sheathed bodies slick as seals
    Loosen and tingle;
And by the board the bare foot feels
    The suck of shingle.

They paddle in the shallows still;
    Two splash each other;
Then all swim out to wait until
    The right waves gather.

The Rooftop

White houses bank the hill,
Facing me where I sit.
It should be adequate
To watch the gardens fill

With sunlight, washing tree,
Bush, and the year's last flowers,
And to sit here for hours,
Becoming what I see.

Perception gave me this:
A whole world, bit by bit.
Yet I can not grasp it—
Bits, not an edifice.

Long webs float on the air.
Glistening, they fall and lift.
I turn it down, the gift:
Such fragile lights can tear.

The heat frets earth already,
Harrowed by furious root;
The wireworm takes his loot;
The midday sun is steady.

Petals turn brown and splay:
Loose in a central shell
Seeds whitening dry and swell
Which light fills from decay.

Ruthless in clean unknowing
The plant obeys its need,
And works alone. The seed
Bursts, bare as bone in going,

Bouncing from rot toward earth,
Compound of rot, to wait,
An armoured concentrate
Containing its own birth.

An unseen edifice.
The seen, the tangles, lead
From seed to death to seed
Through green closed passages.

The light drains from the hill.
The gardens rustle, cold,
Huddled in dark, and hold,
Waiting for when they fill.

Listening to Jefferson Airplane

in the Polo Grounds, Golden Gate Park

The music comes and goes on the wind,
Comes and goes on the brain.

Flooded Meadows

In sunlight now, after the weeks it rained,
Water has mapped irregular shapes that follow
Between no banks, impassive where it drained
Then stayed to rise and brim from every hollow.
Hillocks are firm, though soft, and not yet mud.
Tangles of long bright grass, like waterweed,
Surface upon the patches of the flood,
Distinct as islands from their valleys freed
And sharp as reefs dividing inland seas.
Yet definition is suspended, for,
In pools across the level listlessness,
Light answers only light before the breeze,
Cancelling the rutted, weedy, slow brown floor
For the unity of unabsorbed excess.

Grasses

Laurel and eucalyptus, dry sharp smells,
Pause in the dust of summer. But we sit
High on a fort, above grey blocks and wells,
And watch the restless grasses lapping it.

Each dulling-green, keen, streaky blade of grass
Leans to one body when the breezes start:
A one-time pathway flickers as they pass,
Where paler toward the root the quick ranks part.

The grasses quiver, rising from below.
I wait on warm rough concrete, I have time.
They round off all the lower steps, and blow
Like lights on bended water as they climb.

From some dark passage in the abandoned fort,
I hear a friend's harmonica—withdrawn sound,
A long whine drawling after several short . . .
The spiky body mounting from the ground.

A wail uneven all the afternoon,
Thin, slow, no noise of tramping nor of dance.
It is the sound, half tuneless and half tune,
With which the scattered details make advance.

Kirby's Cove

At the Centre

1

What place is this
                    Cracked wood steps led me here.
The gravelled roof is fenced in where I stand.
But it is open, I am not confined
By weathered boards or barbed wire at the stair,
From which rust crumbles black-red on my hand.
If it is mine. It looks too dark and lined.

What sky
                    A pearly damp grey covers it
Almost infringing on the lighted sign
Above Hamm's Brewery, a huge blond glass
Filling as its component lights are lit.
You cannot keep them. Blinking line by line
They brim beyond the scaffold they replace.

2

What is this steady pouring that
                                          Oh, wonder.
The blue line bleeds and on the gold one draws.
Currents of image widen, braid, and blend
—Pouring in cascade over me and under—
To one all-river. Fleet it does not pause,
The sinewy flux pours without start or end.

What place is this
                    And what is it that broods
Barely beyond its own creation's course,
And not abstracted from it, not the Word,
But overlapping like the wet low clouds
The rivering images—their unstopped source,
Its roar unheard from being always heard.

What am
          Though in the river, I abstract
Fence, word, and notion. On the stream at full
A flurry, where the mind rides separate!
But this brief cresting, sharpened and exact,
Is fluid too, is open to the pull
And on the underside twined deep with it.

3

Terror and beauty in a single board.
The rough grain in relief—a tracery
Fronded and ferned, of woods inside the wood.
Splinter and scar—I saw them too, they poured.
White paint-chip and the overhanging sky:
The flow-lines faintly traced or understood.

Later, downstairs and at the kitchen table,
I look round at my friends. Through light we move
Like foam. We started choosing long ago
—Clearly and capably as we were able—
Hostages from the pouring we are of.
The faces are as bright now as fresh snow.

LSD, Folsom Street

The Discovery of the Pacific

They lean against the cooling car, backs pressed
Upon the dust of a brown continent,
And watch the sun, now Westward of their West,
Fall to the ocean. Where it led they went.

Kansas to California. Day by day
They travelled emptier of the things they knew.
They improvised new habits on the way,
But lost the occasions, and then lost them too.

One night, no one and nowhere, she had woken
To resin-smell and to the firs' slight sound,
And through their sleeping-bag had felt the broken
Tight-knotted surfaces of the naked ground.

Only his lean quiet body cupping hers
Kept her from it, the extreme chill. By degrees
She fell asleep. Around them in the firs
The wind probed, tiding through forked estuaries.

And now their skin is caked with road, the grime
Merely reflecting sunlight as it fails.
They leave their clothes among the rocks they climb,
Blunt leaves of iceplant nuzzle at their soles.

Now they stand chin-deep in the sway of ocean,
Firm West, two stringy bodies face to face,
And come, together, in the water's motion,
The full caught pause of their embrace.

Sunlight

Some things, by their affinity light's token,
Are more than shown: steel glitters from a track;
Small glinting scoops, after a wave has broken,
Dimple the water in its draining back;

Water, glass, metal, match light in their raptures,
Flashing their many answers to the one.
What captures light belongs to what it captures:
The whole side of a world facing the sun,

Re-turned to woo the original perfection,
Giving itself to what created it,
And wearing green in sign of its subjection.
It is as if the sun were infinite.

But angry flaws are swallowed by the distance;
It varies, moves, its concentrated fires
Are slowly dying—the image of persistence
Is an image, only, of our own desires:

Desires and knowledge touch without relating.
The system of which sun and we are part
Is both imperfect and deteriorating.
And yet the sun outlasts us at the heart.

Great seedbed, yellow centre of the flower,
Flower on its own, without a root or stem,
Giving all colour and all shape their power,
Still recreating in defining them,

Enable us, altering like you, to enter
Your passionless love, impartial but intense,
And kindle in acceptance round your centre,
Petals of light lost in your innocence.

from **JACK STRAW'S CASTLE** (1976)

The Bed

The pulsing stops where time has been,
    The garden is snow-bound,
The branches weighed down and the paths filled in,
      Drifts quilt the ground.

We lie soft-caught, still now it's done,
    Loose-twined across the bed
Like wrestling statues; but it still goes on
      Inside my head.

The Night Piece

The fog drifts slowly down the hill
And as I mount gets thicker still,
Closes me in, makes me its own
Like bedclothes on the paving stone.

Here are the last few streets to climb,
Galleries, run through veins of time,
Almost familiar, where I creep
Toward sleep like fog, through fog like sleep.

Last Days at Teddington

The windows wide through day and night
Gave on the garden like a room.
The garden smell, green composite,
Flowed in and out a house in bloom.

To the shaggy dog who skidded from
The concrete through the kitchen door
To yellow-squared linoleum,
It was an undivided floor.

How green it was indoors. The thin
Pale creepers climbed up brick until
We saw their rolled tongues flicker in
Across the cracked paint of the sill.

How sociable the garden was.
We ate and talked in given light.
The children put their toys to grass
All the warm wakeful August night.

So coming back from drinking late
We picked our way below the wall
But in the higher grass, dewed wet,
Stumbled on tricycle and ball.

When everything was moved away,
The house returned to board and shelf,
And smelt of hot dust through the day,
The garden fell back on itself.

All Night, Legs Pointed East

All night, legs pointed east, I shift around
Inside myself, to breast to crotch to head.
Or freed from catnaps to the teeming night
I float, and pinpoint the minutest sound.
I don't know why I doze my time in bed.

An air moves in, I catch the damp plain smells.
But outside, after winter's weeks of rain
The soil of gardens breaks and dries a bit:
A trough between two San Francisco hills
Where granules hold warmth round them as they drain.

Tonight reminds me of my teens in spring—
Not sexual really, it's a plant's unrest
Or bird's expectancy, that enters full
On its conditions, quick eye claw and wing
Submitting to its pulse, alert in the nest.

Toward the night's end the body lies back, still,
Caught in mid-turn by sleep however brief.
In stealth I fill and fill it out. At dawn
Like loosened soil that packs a grassy hill
I fill it wholly, here, hungry for leaf.

Autobiography

The sniff of the real, that's
what I'd want to get
        how it felt
to sit on Parliament
Hill on a May evening
studying for exams   skinny
seventeen   dissatisfied
        yet sniffing such
a potent air, smell of
grass in heat from
the day's sun

I'd been walking through the damp
rich ways by the ponds
and now lay on the upper
grass with Lamartine's poems

life seemed all
loss, and what was more
I'd lost whatever it was
before I'd even had it

a green dry prospect
distant babble of children
and beyond, distinct at
the end of the glow
St. Paul's like a stone thimble

longing so hard to make
inclusions that the longing
has become   in memory
an inclusion

from **THE PASSAGES OF JOY** (1982)

Song of a Camera

for Robert Mapplethorpe

I cut the sentence
out of a life
out of the story
with my little knife

Each bit I cut
shows one alone
dressed or undressed
young full-grown

Look at the bits
He eats he cries
Look at the way
he stands he dies

so that another
seeing the bits
and seeing how
none of them fits

wants to add
adverbs to verbs
A bit on its own
simply disturbs

Wants to say
as well as see
wants to say
valiantly

interpreting
some look in the eyes
a triumph mixed up
with surprise

I cut this sentence
look again
for cowardice
boredom pain

Find what you seek
find what you fear
and be assured
nothing is here

I am the eye
that cut the life
you stand you lie
I am the knife

Keats at Highgate

A cheerful youth joined Coleridge on his walk
("Loose," noted Coleridge, "slack, and not well-dressed")
Listening respectfully to the talk talk talk
Of First and Second Consciousness, then pressed
The famous hand with warmth and sauntered back
Homeward in his own state of less dispersed
More passive consciousness—passive, not slack,
Whether of Secondary type or First.

He made his way toward Hampstead so alert
He hardly passed the small grey ponds below
Or watched a sparrow pecking in the dirt
Without some insight swelling the mind's flow
That banks made swift. Everything put to use.
Perhaps not well-dressed but oh no not loose.

June

In these two separate rooms we sit,
I at my work, you at yours.
I am at once buried in it
And sensible of all outdoors.

The month is cool, as if on guard,
High fog holds back the sky for days,
But in their sullen patch of yard
The Oriental Poppies blaze.

Separate in the same weather
The parcelled buds crack pink and red,
And rise from different plants together
To shed their bud-sheaths on the bed,

And stretch their crumpled petals free,
That nurse the box of hardening seed,
In the same hour, as if to agree
On what could not have been agreed.

from **THE MAN WITH NIGHT SWEATS** (1992)

The Hug

It was your birthday, we had drunk and dined
  Half of the night with our old friend
    Who'd showed us in the end
  To a bed I reached in one drunk stride.
    Already I lay snug,
And drowsy with the wine dozed on one side.

I dozed, I slept. My sleep broke on a hug,
    Suddenly, from behind,
In which the full lengths of our bodies pressed:
    Your instep to my heel,
  My shoulder-blades against your chest.
  It was not sex, but I could feel
  The whole strength of your body set,
    Or braced, to mine,
    And locking me to you
  As if we were still twenty-two
  When our grand passion had not yet
    Become familial.
  My quick sleep had deleted all
  Of intervening time and place.
    I only knew
The stay of your secure firm dry embrace.

To a Friend in Time of Trouble

You wake tired, in the cabin light has filled,
Then walk out to the deck you helped to build,
And pause, your senses reaching out anxiously,
Tentatively, toward scrub and giant tree:
A giving of the self instructed by
The dog who settles near you with a sigh
And seeks you in your movements, following each.
Though yours are different senses, they too reach
Until you know that they engage the air
—The clean and penetrable medium where
You encounter as if they were a sort of home
Fountains of fern that jet from the coarse loam.

You listen for the quiet, but hear instead
A sudden run of cries break overhead,
And look to see a wide-winged bird of prey
Between the redwood tops carrying away
Some small dark bundle outlined in its claws.
The certainty, the ease with which it draws
Its arc on blue . . . Soon the protesting shriek,
The gorging from the breast, the reddened beak,
The steadying claw withdrawn at last. You know
It is not cruel, it is not human, though
You cringe who would not feel surprised to find
Such lacerations made by mind on mind.

Later, the job, you haul large stones uphill.
You intend to pile them in a wall which will,
In front of plantings and good dirt, retain
Through many a winter of eroding rain.
Hard work and tiring, but the exercise
Opens the blood to air and simplifies
The memory of your troubles in the city,
Until you view them unconfused by pity.

A handsome grey-haired, grey-eyed man, tight-knit;
Each muscle clenching as you call on it
From the charmed empire of your middle age.
You move about your chores: the grief and rage
You brought out here begin at last to unbind.
And all day as you climb, the released mind
Unclenches till—the moment of release
Clean overlooked in the access of its own peace—
It finds that it has lost itself upon
The smooth red body of a young madrone,
From which it turns toward other varying shades
On the brown hillside where light grows and fades,
And feels the healing start, and still returns,
Riding its own repose, and learns, and learns.

Philemon and Baucis

love without shadows—W.C.W.

Two trunks like bodies, bodies like twined trunks
Supported by their wooden hug. Leaves shine
In tender habit at the extremities.
Truly each other's, they have embraced so long
Their barks have met and wedded in one flow
Blanketing both. Time lights the handsome bulk.
    The gods were grateful, and for comfort given
Gave comfort multiplied a thousandfold.
Therefore the couple leached into that soil
The differences prolonged through their late vigour
That kept their exchanges salty and abrasive,
And found, with loves balancing equally,
Full peace of mind. They put unease behind them
A long time back, a long time back forgot
How each woke separate through the pale grey night,
A long time back forgot the days when each
—Riding the other's nervous exuberance—
Knew the slow thrill of learning how to love
What, gradually revealed, becomes itself,
Expands, unsheathes, as the keen rays explore:
Invented in the continuous revelation.

They have drifted into a perpetual nap,
The peace of trees that all night whisper nothings.

A Sketch of the Great Dejection

Having read the promise of the hedgerow
the body set out anew on its adventures.
At length it came to a place of poverty,
of inner and outer famine,
        where all movement had stopped
except for that of the wind, which was continual
and came from elsewhere, from the sea,
moving across unplanted fields and between headstones
in the little churchyard clogged with nettles
where no one came between Sundays, and few then.
The wind was like a punishment to the face and hands.
These were marshes of privation:
the mud of the ditches oozed scummy water,
the grey reeds were arrested in growth,
the sun did not show, even as a blur,
and the uneven lands were without definition
as I was without potent words,
inert.

      I sat upon a disintegrating gravestone.
How can I continue? I asked.
I longed to whet my senses, but upon what?
On mud? It was a desert of raw mud.
I was tempted by fantasies of the past,
but my body rejected them, for only in the present
could it pursue the promise,
        keeping open to its fulfilment.
I would not, either, sink into the mud,
warming it with the warmth I brought to it,
        as in a sty of sloth.
My body insisted on restlessness
        having been promised love,
as my mind insisted on words
        having been promised the imagination.

So I remained alert, confused and uncomforted.
I fared on and, though the landscape did not change,
it came to seem after a while like a place of recuperation.

Patch Work

The bird book says, common, conspicuous.
This time of year all day
The mockingbird
Sweeps at a moderate height
Above the densely flowering
Suburban plots of May,
The characteristic shine
Of white patch cutting through the curved ash-grey
That bars each wing;
Or it appears to us
Perched on the post that ends a washing-line
To sing there, as in flight,
A repertoire of songs that it has heard
—From other birds, and others of its kind—
Which it has recombined
And made its own, especially one
With a few separate plangent notes begun
Then linking trills as a long confident run
Toward the immediate distance,
Repeated all day through
In the sexual longings of the spring
(Which also are derivative)
And almost mounting to
Fulfilment, thus to give
Such muscular vigour to a note so strong,
Fulfilment that does not destroy
The original, still-unspent
Longings that led it where it went
But links them in a bird's inhuman joy
Lifted upon the wing
Of that patched body, that insistence
Which fills the gardens up with headlong song.

Well Dennis O'Grady

Well Dennis O'Grady
said the smiling old woman
pausing at the bus stop I hear
they are still praying for you
I read it in the Bulletin.

His wattle throat sagged
above his careful tie and clean brown suit.
I didn't hear his answer,
but though bent a bit
over his stick
he was delighted to be out
in the slight December sunshine
—having a good walk, pleased
it seems at all the prayers
and walking pretty straight
on his own.

The Stealer

I lie and live
my body's fear
something's at large
and coming near

No deadbolt
can keep it back
A worm of fog
leaks through a crack

From the darkness
as before
it grows to body
in my door

Like a taker
scarved and gloved
it steals this way
like one I loved

Fear stiffens me
and a slow joy
at the approach
of the sheathed boy

Will he too do
what that one did
unlock me first
open the lid

and reach inside
with playful feel
all the better
thus to steal

Nasturtium

Born in a sour waste lot
You laboured up to light,
Bunching what strength you'd got
And running out of sight
Through a knot-hole at last,
To come forth into sun
As if without a past,
Done with it, re-begun.

Now street-side of the fence
You take a few green turns,
Nimble in nonchalance
Before your first flower burns.
From poverty and prison
And undernourishment
A prodigal has risen,
Self-spending, never spent.

Irregular yellow shell
And drooping spur behind . . .
Not rare but beautiful
—Street-handsome—as you wind
And leap, hold after hold,
A golden runaway
Still running, strewing gold
From side to side all day.

The Man with Night Sweats

I wake up cold, I who
Prospered through dreams of heat
Wake to their residue,
Sweat, and a clinging sheet.

My flesh was its own shield:
Where it was gashed, it healed.

I grew as I explored
The body I could trust
Even while I adored
The risk that made robust,

A world of wonders in
Each challenge to the skin.

I cannot but be sorry
The given shield was cracked
My mind reduced to hurry,
My flesh reduced and wrecked.

I have to change the bed,
But catch myself instead

Stopped upright where I am
Hugging my body to me
As if to shield it from
The pains that will go through me,

As if hands were enough
To hold an avalanche off.

Lament

Your dying was a difficult enterprise.
First, petty things took up your energies,
The small but clustering duties of the sick,
Irritant as the cough's dry rhetoric.
Those hours of waiting for pills, shot, X-ray
Or test (while you read novels two a day)
Already with a kind of clumsy stealth
Distanced you from the habits of your health.
   In hope still, courteous still, but tired and thin,
You tried to stay the man that you had been,
Treating each symptom as a mere mishap
Without import. But then the spinal tap.
It brought a hard headache, and when night came
I heard you wake up from the same bad dream
Every half-hour with the same short cry
Of mild outrage, before immediately
Slipping into the nightmare once again
Empty of content but the drip of pain.
No respite followed: though the nightmare ceased,
Your cough grew thick and rich, its strength increased.
Four nights, and on the fifth we drove you down
To the Emergency Room. That frown, that frown:
I'd never seen such rage in you before
As when they wheeled you through the swinging door.
For you knew, rightly, they conveyed you from
Those normal pleasures of the sun's kingdom
The hedonistic body basks within
And takes for granted—summer on the skin,
Sleep without break, the moderate taste of tea
In a dry mouth. You had gone on from me
As if your body sought our martyrdom
In the far Canada of a hospital room.
Once there, you entered fully the distress

And long pale rigours of the wilderness.
A gust of morphine hid you. Back in sight
You breathed through a segmented tube, fat, white,
Jammed down your throat so that you could not speak.
    How thin the distance made you. In your cheek
One day, appeared the true shape of your bone
No longer padded. Still your mind, alone,
Explored this emptying intermediate
State for what holds and rests were hidden in it.
    You wrote us messages on a pad, amused
At one time that you had your nurse confused
Who, seeing you reconciled after four years
With your grey father, both of you in tears,
Asked if this was at last your "special friend"
(The one you waited for until the end).
"She sings," you wrote, "a Philippine folk song
To wake me in the morning . . . It is long
And very pretty." Grabbing at detail
To furnish this bare ledge toured by the gale,
On which you lay, bed restful as a knife,
You tried, tried hard, to make of it a life
Thick with the complicating circumstance
Your thoughts might fasten on. It had been chance
Always till now that had filled up the moment
With live specifics your hilarious comment
Discovered as it went along; and fed,
Laconic, quick, wherever it was led.
You improvised upon your own delight.
I think back to the scented summer night
We talked between our sleeping bags, below
A molten field of stars five years ago:
I was so tickled by your mind's light touch
I couldn't sleep, you made me laugh too much,
Though I was tired and begged you to leave off.

Now you were tired, and yet not tired enough
—Still hungry for the great world you were losing
Steadily in no season of your choosing—
And when at last the whole death was assured,
Drugs having failed, and when you had endured
Two weeks of an abominable constraint,
You faced it equably, without complaint,
Unwhimpering, but not at peace with it.
You'd lived as if your time was infinite:
You were not ready and not reconciled,
Feeling as uncompleted as a child
Till you had shown the world what you could do
In some ambitious role to be worked through,
A role your need for it had half-defined,
But never wholly, even in your mind.
You lacked the necessary ruthlessness,
The soaring meanness that pinpoints success.
We loved that lack of self-love, and your smile,
Rueful, at your own silliness.
                                        Meanwhile,
Your lungs collapsed, and the machine, unstrained,
Did all your breathing now. Nothing remained
But death by drowning on an inland sea
Of your own fluids, which it seemed could be
Kindly forestalled by drugs. Both could and would:
Nothing was said, everything understood,
At least by us. Your own concerns were not
Long-term, precisely, when they gave the shot
—You made local arrangements to the bed
And pulled a pillow round beside your head.
    And so you slept, and died, your skin gone grey,
Achieving your completeness, in a way.

Outdoors next day, I was dizzy from a sense
Of being ejected with some violence

From vigil in a white and distant spot
Where I was numb, into this garden plot
Too warm, too close, and not enough like pain.
I was delivered into time again
—The variations that I live among
Where your long body too used to belong
And where the still bush is minutely active.
You never thought your body was attractive,
Though others did, and yet you trusted it
And must have loved its fickleness a bit
Since it was yours and gave you what it could,
Till near the end it let you down for good,
Its blood hospitable to those guests who
Took over by betraying it into
The greatest of its inconsistencies
This difficult, tedious, painful enterprise.

Still Life

I shall not soon forget
The greyish-yellow skin
To which the face had set:
Lids tight: nothing of his,
No tremor from within,
Played on the surfaces.

He still found breath, and yet
It was an obscure knack.
I shall not soon forget
The angle of his head,
Arrested and reared back
On the crisp field of bed,

Back from what he could neither
Accept, as one opposed,
Nor, as a life-long breather,
Consentingly let go,
The tube his mouth enclosed
In an astonished O.

The J Car

Last year I used to ride the J CHURCH Line,
Climbing between small yards recessed with vine
—Their ordered privacy, their plots of flowers
Like blameless lives we might imagine ours.
Most trees were cut back, but some brushed the car
Before it swung round to the street once more
On which I rolled out almost to the end,
To 29th Street, calling for my friend.
    He'd be there at the door, smiling but gaunt,
To set out for the German restaurant.
There, since his sight was tattered now, I would
First read the menu out. He liked the food
In which a sourness and dark richness meet
For conflict without taste of a defeat,
As in the Sauerbraten. What he ate
I hoped would help him to put on some weight,
But though the crusted pancakes might attract
They did so more as concept than in fact,
And I'd eat his dessert before we both
Rose from the neat arrangement of the cloth,
Where the connection between life and food
Had briefly seemed so obvious if so crude.
Our conversation circumspectly cheerful,
We had sat here like children good but fearful
Who think if they behave everything might
Still against likelihood come out all right.
    But it would not, and we could not stay here:
Finishing up the Optimator beer
I walked him home through the suburban cool
By dimming shape of church and Catholic school,
Only a few, white, teenagers about.
After the four blocks he would be tired out.
I'd leave him to the feverish sleep ahead,
Myself to ride through darkened yards instead

Back to my health. Of course I simplify.
Of course. It tears me still that he should die
As only an apprentice to his trade,
The ultimate engagements not yet made.
His gifts had been withdrawing one by one
Even before their usefulness was done:
This optic nerve would never be relit;
The other flickered, soon to be with it.
Unready, disappointed, unachieved,
He knew he would not write the much-conceived
Much-hoped-for work now, nor yet help create
A love he might in full reciprocate.

The Missing

Now as I watch the progress of the plague,
The friends surrounding me fall sick, grow thin,
And drop away. Bared, is my shape less vague
—Sharply exposed and with a sculpted skin?

I do not like the statue's chill contour,
Not nowadays. The warmth investing me
Led outward through mind, limb, feeling, and more
In an involved increasing family.

Contact of friend led to another friend,
Supple entwinement through the living mass
Which for all that I knew might have no end,
Image of an unlimited embrace.

I did not just feel ease, though comfortable:
Aggressive as in some ideal of sport,
With ceaseless movement thrilling through the whole,
Their push kept me as firm as their support.

But death—Their deaths have left me less defined:
It was their pulsing presence made me clear.
I borrowed from it, I was unconfined,
Who tonight balance unsupported here,

Eyes glaring from raw marble, in a pose
Languorously part-buried in the block,
Shins perfect and no calves, as if I froze
Between potential and a finished work.

—Abandoned incomplete, shape of a shape,
In which exact detail shows the more strange,
Trapped in unwholeness, I find no escape
Back to the play of constant give and change.

August 1987

Death's Door

Of course the dead outnumber us
—How their recruiting armies grow!
My mother archaic now as Minos,
She who died forty years ago.

After their processing, the dead
Sit down in groups and watch TV,
In which they must be interested,
For on it they see you and me.

These four, who though they never met
Died in one month, sit side by side
Together in front of the same set,
And all without a *TV Guide*.

Arms round each other's shoulders loosely,
Although they can feel nothing, who
When they unlearned their pain so sprucely
Let go of all sensation too.

Thus they watch friend and relative
And life here as they think it is
—In black and white, repetitive
As situation comedies.

With both delight and tears at first
They greet each programme on death's stations,
But in the end lose interest,
Their boredom turning to impatience.

"He misses me? He must be kidding
—This week he's sleeping with a cop."
"All she reads now is *Little Gidding*."
"They're getting old. I wish they'd stop."

The habit of companionship
Lapses—they break themselves of touch:
Edging apart at arm and hip,
Till separated on the couch,

They woo amnesia, look away
As if they were not yet elsewhere,
And when snow blurs the picture they,
Turned, give it a belonging stare.

Snow blows out toward them, till their seat
Filling with flakes becomes instead
Snow-bank, snow-landscape, and in that
They find themselves with all the dead,

Where passive light from snow-crust shows them
Both Minos circling and my mother.
Yet none of the recruits now knows them,
Nor do they recognize each other,

They have been so superbly trained
Into the perfect discipline
Of an archaic host, and weaned
From memory briefly barracked in.

from **BOSS CUPID** (2000)

My Mother's Pride

She dramatized herself
Without thought of the dangers.
But "Never pay attention," she said,
"To the opinions of strangers."

And when I stole from a counter,
"You wouldn't accept a present
From a tradesman." But I think I might have:
I had the greed of a peasant.

She was proud of her ruthless wit
And the smallest ears in London.
"Only conceited children are shy."
I am made by her, and undone.

The Gas-poker

Forty-eight years ago
—Can it be forty-eight
Since then?—they forced the door
Which she had barricaded
With a full bureau's weight
Lest anyone find, as they did,
What she had blocked it for.

She had blocked the doorway so,
To keep the children out.
In her red dressing-gown
She wrote notes, all night busy
Pushing the things about,
Thinking till she was dizzy,
Before she had lain down.

The children went to and fro
On the harsh winter lawn
Repeating their lament,
A burden, to each other
In the December dawn,
Elder and younger brother,
Till they knew what it meant.

Knew all there was to know.
Coming back off the grass
To the room of her release,
They who had been her treasures
Knew to turn off the gas,
Take the appropriate measures,
Telephone the police.

One image from the flow
Sticks in the stubborn mind:
A sort of backwards flute.
The poker that she held up
Breathed from the holes aligned
Into her mouth till, filled up
By its music, she was mute.

Arachne

What is that bundle hanging from the ceiling
Unresting even now with constant slight
Drift in the breeze that breathes through rooms at night?
Can it be something, then, that once had feeling,
A girl, perhaps, whose skill and pride and hope
Strangled against each other in the rope?

I think it is a tangle of despair
As shapeless as a bit of woven nest,
Blackened and matted, quivering without rest
At the mercy of the movements of the air
Where half-lodged in, half-fallen from the hedge
It hangs tormented at a season's edge.

What an exact artificer she had been!
Her daintiness and firmness are reduced
To lumpy shadow that the dark has noosed.
Something is changing, though. Movements begin
Obscurely as the court of night adjourns,
A tiny busyness at the centre turns.

So she spins who was monarch of the loom,
Reduced indeed, but she lets out a fine
And delicate yet tough and tensile line
That catches full day in the little room,
Then sways minutely, suddenly out of sight,
And then again the thread invents the light.

Shit

an essay on Rimbaud

The marvellous boy, in his sweet sticky ardor,
Grabbed M. Paul beneath the café table
And growing harder (his poetry grew harder)
Pumped him as thoroughly as he was able.

The older poet, master of sweet sounds,
Couldn't keep up with all this penile strumming
Of the enthusiastic vagabond's.
He always felt religious after coming.

The boy was bolder. Hair crawling with lice,
Smoked a foul pipe, it was deliberate,
Cracked poetry readings open, far from nice,
His favorite saying shit, and he meant shit.

Coursed after meaning, meaning of course to trick it,
Across the lush green meadows of his youth,
To the edge of the unintelligible thicket
Where truth becomes the same place as untruth,

And trapped it between the two, awful suspension,
Its whiskers quivering through the Romantic mist,
In terror that had stripped it of intention.
He was as cool as a vivisectionist.

For then he ate it, he ate meaning live,
Ate all provincial France, the pasturing herd
And village-girls he once had thought to wive.
His shit was poetry: alchemy of the word.

He levitated, swooning from sheer power.
"Only I have the key," he came to state,
Dreaming that he had reached the highest tower,
But woke on hard stones. Those he also ate.

Till in the end he lost words; and his faeces
Came just from what he ate with fork and knife;
And subsequently too he fell to pieces,
Losing a leg here, there a life.

The Dump

He died, and I admired
the crisp vehemence
of a lifetime reduced to
half a foot of shelf space.
But others came to me saying,
we too loved him,
let us take you to
the place of our love.
So they showed me
everything, everything—
a cliff of notebooks
with every draft and erasure
of every poem he
published or rejected,
thatched already
with webs of annotation.
I went in further and saw
a hill of matchcovers
from every bar or restaurant
he'd ever entered. Trucks
backed up constantly,
piled with papers, awaited
by archivists with shovels;
forklifts bumped through
trough and valley
to adjust the spillage.
Here odors of rubbery sweat
intruded on the pervasive
smell of stale paper,
no doubt from the mound
of his collected sneakers.
I clambered up the highest
pile and found myself
looking across not history

but the vistas of a steaming
range of garbage
reaching to the coast itself. Then
I lost my footing! and was
carried down on a soft
avalanche of letters, paid bills,
sexual polaroids, and notes
refusing invitations, thanking
fans, resisting scholars.
In nightmare I slid,
no ground to stop me,

until I woke at last
where I had napped beside
the precious half-foot. Beyond that,
nothing, nothing at all.

In Trust

You go from me
In June for months on end
To study equanimity
Among high trees alone;
I go out with a new boyfriend
And stay all summer in the city where
Home mostly on my own
I watch the sunflowers flare.

You travel East
To help your relatives.
The rainy season's start, at least,
Brings you from banishment:
And from the hall a doorway gives
A glimpse of you, writing I don't know what,
Through winter, with head bent
In the lamp's yellow spot.

To some fresh task
Some improvising skill
Your face is turned, of which I ask
Nothing except the presence:
Beneath white hair your clear eyes still
Are candid as the cat's fixed narrowing gaze
—Its pale-blue incandescence
In your room nowadays.

Sociable cat:
Without much noise or fuss
We left the kitchen where he sat,
And suddenly we find
He happens still to be with us,
In this room now, though firmly faced away,
Not to be left behind,
Though all the night he'll stray.

As you began
You'll end the year with me.
We'll hug each other while we can,
Work or stray while we must.
Nothing is, or will ever be,
Mine, I suppose. No one can hold a heart,
But what we hold in trust
We do hold, even apart.

West Tisbury Free Public Library

0 7000 0189231 9

DATE DUE

APR 0 6 2009

APR 2 2 2009
MAY 0 9 2009
SEP 0 9 2009
NOV 1 6 2009
NOV 2 3 2009
MAR 1 8 2010
APR 2 0 2010

WITHDRAWN

GAYLORD   PRINTED IN U.S.A.